KIM McGOURTY

Unsave THE Date

ARE YOU WIFE READY?

Preparing Women for Marriage Beyond the Wedding Day

Unsave the Date: Are You Wife Ready?
Preparing women for marriage beyond the wedding day
Copyright ©2018

MoniMar Publishing
110 Walter Way, Suite #1751
Stockbridge, GA 30281
www.wifeready.org
kim.mcquitty@gmail.com

ISBN: 978-0-69215-881-4

Unless otherwise indicated, all Scripture is taken from the King James Version of the Bible.

Scriptural quotations taken from the New American Standard Bible® (NASB)

Copyright © 1960, 1962, 1963, 1968, 1971, 1972, 1973, 1975, 1977, 1995 by The Lockman Foundation. Used by permission. www.Lockman.org

Cover, author's photograph, and interior design by Marielle McQuitty. www.mariellemcquitty.com

Printed in the United States of America

in loving memory of my late husband,
marvin n. mcQuitty, jr.

contents

introduction

This book is written from the vantage point of capturing everything I would want you to know if you were one of my premarital counseling clients, sitting on the sofa in my office or at a local coffee shop. Contained herein is everything I wish women knew before making the big decisions about love, life and marriage.

Be it from when you were a young girl or perhaps later in your mature years, you have developed a desire to be married. To that, I say what a wonderful desire to have. I believe the longing for, the desire to be, and the dream of being married comes from God. After all, He created a plan for a church that He refers to as His bride. We are created relational beings by the One who desires a relationship with us. It makes perfect sense, then, that many of us want deep connections with family, friends, and even a mate. Yet, simply having the desire isn't enough. When it comes to marriage, much more is necessary, and much more required.

It is important that you know and understand what it takes to be fully whole, healed, and prepared to have not just the wedding ceremony you've dreamed of, but also to create a marriage relationship that will last and be fulfilling. There is a plan for your happiness even in marriage.

Marriage is not about flowers, saying yes to the dress, the perfect venue, or how few or how many carats your ring is. It's not about clever hashtags and witty social media posts. Marriage is a commitment made before God for the rest of your life to join purpose, visions, and goals. It is embarking on a joint journey with steps and stops ordained by God Himself. He intended marriage to be the joining of two people to fulfill a combined purpose. Marriage will be full of love and companionship. It shouldn't be taken lightly, but reverently and discreetly, as the minister will tell you on your wedding day.

To be honest, as a young woman getting married, I wished marriage was as easy as picking a color palate and cake flavor. I'd love to tell you that you've made it just because you were proposed to or you selected your wedding song. Being successfully married will require more work and sacrifice than you've ever imagined. A loving, Christ-centered marriage will stretch you in ways you never thought possible. But there are certainly ways through which we can prepare ourselves.

What I have discovered from women who have been married for some time is that one of their primary wishes is that they had known that part of the work of a good marriage was about themselves. Overcoming issues from their past; having the maturity, fortitude, and mindset to be someone's wife; being mentally, emotionally, and spiritually willing to work through current issues that may arise; are all a part of the work.

So, are you ready? Because to get to the work of marriage, there's some work you need to do beforehand. God doesn't want half of you marrying half of your fiancé. He wants fully you marrying fully him.

I married my husband at the age of 20 years old. The lack of maturity and life experiences placed me at a disadvantage from the start. Many of the challenges, and things I did or didn't do, stemmed from my immaturity and lack of marital readiness. I learned through trial and error and the school of hard knocks how to be a wife. My hope is that this writing will help you avoid that particular route.

The best times of my life were being married and being a mom. I loved having someone in the world who cared as deeply for me as I did for him. I can attribute some of the most life-giving, memorable, and fulfilling moments of my life so far to being Marvin McQuitty's wife and, of course, to my role as a mother.

When I got married, it was forever. I thought we'd grow old together. Life, though, has a way of interrupting even the best of plans. Sometimes our hopes are shattered, and our dreams die heartbreaking deaths. Unbeknownst to either of us, when I married my husband, he had already lived half of his life. On September 11, 2012 at the age of 46, he passed away. I loved him deeply. He was my friend and confidant, as well as a wonderful husband and father. I loved being married to him.

After 24 years of marriage, I can honestly say I have few regrets. By no means was I perfect in any way. I made countless mistakes. I had to submit myself to the process of inner healing and forgiveness many times. I grappled with the question of whether I married "the right one" when things got tough. (I share the journey of our lives together in my book, *Me, My Man and His Music: My Life as a Musician's Wife*). In the process of my marriage, after years of doing it my way, I finally allowed the Lord to work His will in me as I surrendered my plans and purpose for my marriage to His plans.

In the chapters that follow, I will challenge many of your thoughts and beliefs on marriage, ask you some hard questions, and share real life stories. If you go through this entire book fully embracing all that is covered, I am certain that some myths will be debunked, healing will take place, a better understanding of yourself will happen, and you will feel more secure. I want to help you become wife ready.

I believe that becoming wife ready is a journey that every woman should take before saying "I do." So what does marital readiness look like? It varies from woman to woman. It is predicated upon your life experiences, chronological age, level of maturity, and the season of life you are currently in.

Wife readiness is when a woman has a clear revelation of God's love for her. She isn't needy in the relationship, trying to fill a God-shaped hole with someone else, because she already knows she is loved deeply and wholly by God. She won't carry insecurities into the relationship, where she's trying to extract love from another person. There won't be a love deficiency, because she knows how powerful, permanent, and perfect God's love is for her. She will be more fulfilled, because her soul is anchored in God's agape love. When a woman fully understands this, she spends a lifetime pouring that love out on others. It is this revelation that changes every relationship, especially in marriage.

Come take this journey with me. Commit to doing the work necessary to become wife ready, and I promise it will be worth it.

are you ready
to work?

1

are you ready to work?

It was my wedding day, and excitement was in the air. I was on Cloud 9 as I prepared to say "I do" to the man of my dreams. The wedding ceremony was scheduled to begin promptly at four o'clock pm. However, I simply could not wait until then to get dressed up. This entire day was all about me, and it promised to be one I would always remember.

Getting dressed for my hair appointment, I chose a white 2-piece suit to wear to the hair salon. Who says you have to wait until you walk down the aisle to wear white? It was my day… the long-awaited day. I would begin the first day of the rest of my life as a wife.

As our wedding guests stood to receive me, my dad and I locked arms and walked toward my husband-to-be. This was the man who would change my last name to his. He was the one with whom I felt safe to share my secrets. This was the man whose children I would bear. It was to this man I was pledging my love; the one with whom I would exchange vows to live and love each other for the rest of our lives.

I always imagined being married and becoming a wife one day. I considered myself "wife material" decades before pop culture deemed it a hashtag on social media.

As a young girl, dreaming and thinking about the future, I looked forward to this day. I was captivated by the thought of marrying my Prince Charming. I had an ideal of marriage but not an actual concept.

I never heard 'hard work' or 'work' of any kind and 'marriage' in the same sentence. If I did, it related to taking care of the home and being a mother. In no way had the concept of work been discussed as what would be necessary every day to become one flesh. Who knew love required work? Isn't it a feeling? Isn't love enough? I was so enamored with and smitten by my man, it never occurred to me that love isn't enough to sustain a marriage. I wasn't ignorant to the challenges that relationships encounter, but I wasn't educated about them either.

Had I known on my wedding day what I know now, I could have navigated my marriage far easier and framed my expectations far better. I would have known as I entered into marriage that it would indeed require work from both of us. It would have helped us greatly to have sought out answers and understanding to some vital questions while we were still dating and engaged. What I discovered over the years of my marriage is that it's not only important to get information, but it is also critical to make sure that the information is received from the proper source.

Everything you'll ever need pertaining to marriage can be found in the Word of God. Marriage is holy and the closest thing that represents our relationship with God on earth. That's why marriage is so important to Him and why it is under attack by the enemy. The enemy hates marriage and will stop at nothing to dissolve yours. You must be armed and ready to fight back.

This level of information would have been invaluable to me on my wedding day and the days, months, and even years leading up to it. To have this awareness as I said the words that would forever change my life, may have made the difference. Looking back, I never truly answered a very important question: Am I ready to work? Work? Love! I was ready for that. But work?

I know what society, my parents, and even my pastor taught and expected of me… that it is appropriate to get married, especially when you feel as deeply as I did about my man. And to be honest, this is not a good enough reason to get married. It is not about fulfilling a lifelong dream, avoiding loneliness, not sinning, or Lifetime movie ideals.

Dr. Tony Evans writes in *Kingdom Woman*, "A biblical understanding of the nature and purpose of the marriage covenant is essential. There is more to marriage than feelings. There is a shared calling to impact the world on behalf of God's Kingdom and to glorify God in all that you do."[1] Marriage is more than no longer being alone and doing life with someone; it's a partnership based on spiritual intimacy and the ability to pursue God together.

I remember, as I arrived at the altar, the peace and euphoria I felt couldn't be articulated. It was the best day of my life! I felt as if I were floating down the aisle. After my dad handed me off to my soon-to-be husband to exchange vows and wedding rings, the ceremony lasted all of 20 minutes. I recall thinking, *"Are you serious? Is this over already?"* Years of dreaming and months of planning were over in a matter of minutes. *"Am I really married that quickly?"* I was. My husband and I had just made a covenant before God. We were on the road to the blessings and benefits that awaited our union. Marriage is a wonderful friendship set to music, and that's a part of our love story.

After the ceremony, we greeted our guests. So many came from around and out of town to witness our nuptials as we began the first day of the rest of our lives together. I can't recall a time before my wedding day when I was happier or more excited. It was *the* best day of my life!

The excitement flowed into the reception, where more of my décor dreams came alive. While enjoying dinner with the backdrop of a live band, we went from table to table speaking with more guests. We really appreciated everyone coming to celebrate with us. Soon after taking the infamous and traditional smashing cake face photo, we were off to take more pictures with our bridal party and family members.

As the evening came to an end, there were mixed emotions—sadness that our day had ended and excitement that my dream of being a wife was coming true. It was then that our journey of husband and wife began, whether we were ready or not.

We left the church in a limousine headed to our honeymoon suite at a local hotel. While waiting to drive off, it hit me that I was married. There were no more do's and don'ts as my husband and I made the commitment to walk in purity. Just like that, we were free to express the love we shared to one another without guilt or shame. It was one of the most rewarding feelings we had, because we honored God in our dating relationship and chose to give the gift of celibacy to each other on our wedding night.

I thought I was in love on my wedding day, and, of course, I was. However, I became more so over the years, as our love grew stronger. Our vows would be tested and tried. Our marriage, although amazing, was not without hardships. Those very hardships enabled us to create a deeper level of intimacy.

Marriage is the best thing next to heaven or the closest thing to hell you will ever experience on earth. I understand that statement is very direct, but what purpose will this book serve if I'm not completely honest and transparent with you?

Your marriage will be based on your past experiences and expectations and herein lies some of the challenges you will face. You are a product of your past and the ideas you have formed about how relationships work. While these ideas and concepts are not bad, some of them will definitely need to be redirected, reworked, reshaped, reconsidered, and removed.

What preconceived notions do you have about marriage? What myths need to be debunked? What lessons has life taught you along the way? Where have you gotten your information? To whom have you looked to for advice or as an example? What have you experienced about relationships? What has worked, and what has failed? These are all questions you should take the time to answer. You didn't pick up this book by accident. Whether you are currently single, single again, a newlywed, dating, or engaged, there is always room to learn something that can make life better. I want to help you through this process by offering you real-life strategies and by challenging what you know.

When the euphoria wears off, that's when the work begins. The "feeling of love" doesn't require much work. It's when those feelings wane that you have to be intentional in keeping love alive. The business of marriage comes easy; deciding who will handle what, but you must work for the romance. Your marriage won't be on ten every day.

So, I ask again, are you ready? In your marriage, there will be victories and defeats, as well as tears and lots of laughter. You will make wonderful memories that will last a lifetime. You are in for some of the best days of your life, in sharing the rest of your life with the love of your life.

Marriage is rewarding and challenging. It takes grit, tenacity, character, sacrifice, courage and humility. It's an undoing and building back again. It requires you to be fearless, brave, and stretched beyond what you ever thought was humanly possible. You will be taken out of your comfort zone and challenged on every side. It takes selflessness and creating boundaries. It requires romance, intimacy, apologies, forgiveness, and grace. It takes discipline, patience, determination, and a tenacity that won't quit.

Your marriage must be a priority at all times. It requires both of you making decisions for the betterment of the relationship. It takes intentionality, financial stewardship, and wise counsel. Marriage requires date nights, encouragement, commitment, faithfulness, and trust. There will be transitions and readjustments. It is two servants aiming to out serve the other. So, I ask again, are you ready? Because marriage, though beautiful, is work!

being engaged is a step, not a status

Dating is a time of intention in getting to know one another and is designed to establish trust. Even though you are putting your best foot forward, you are still determining if this gentleman fits what you are looking for in a lifelong partner. Choosing him will be the second biggest decision you make in your lifetime, with the first being your relationship with Jesus Christ. You can never overthink or over-contemplate your future.

Once you have determined, with the help of the Lord, that the man which you have been dating is who you want to spend the rest of your life with, a proposal and engagement is the next step. This window of time is geared toward preparing for the wedding day. It is not a destination or the end goal!

You should not be walking around for years with a ring on your finger and an ambiguous wedding date. If you are the one who is stalling, do a little self-examination, and ask yourself why you are allowing this to happen. If he's the one who's stalling, why are you allowing him to drag his feet with you in tow?

If a guy knows for one minute you won't put up with his lack of commitment, and he really loves you, he won't let you get away. But if you're stuck in an endless engagement, you haven't required commitment of him or created a fear of loss. That's why he has ended his commitment with just a ring and no ceremony. If you have been engaged indefinitely, ask yourself, why haven't you gotten married yet? Why have you minimized your worth and value to an endless engagement? Take it from me, you are worth so much more!

A while back, I had an opportunity to be interviewed for an upcoming premarital reality television show. While video chatting with one of the producers, she asked me my thoughts on a seven-year engagement. I told her it's one of two reasons or possibly both. First, the young lady doesn't know who she is. A woman who knows her worth and value will not allow her life to hang in the balance indefinitely with a man who will not commit his life to her. She won't allow herself to be a permanent girlfriend under any circumstances and be in an engagement with no wedding date.

The second reason is fear. Fear has so many defining factors and layers it could be any number of reasons why the commitment hasn't been made. A woman would have to do a self-exploration of why she has allowed fear to paralyze her from a wonderful, loving and life-giving relationship like marriage.

Here's something else to explore. It may not be all on you. Is he stalling on the way to the altar? Was he pressured to propose to appease you or his parents? Has he told you that he doesn't want to marry you, and you're just not listening? He may not have said it in those exact words but may have alluded to it by saying things like, "Marriage isn't for everyone," or "Does marriage even work anymore?" or "I'm not the marrying kind." Pay attention, and listen to what he's saying if he continues to delay in moving forward. He may be telling you he doesn't want to be married.

While we are on the subject of being engaged, allow me to address something that has become pervasive in today's society. Instead of progressing in a relationship the way that God intends, many couples are simply cohabitating. Living together for men can be a stall from marriage, and, for women, it's a step towards it. However, statistics say that couples who live together before getting married have a higher divorce rate than those who do not. The likelihood is that they slid into living together instead of deciding to be together.[2] Some couples are together for so long that moving in together seems like the next step when actually it's not.

People who decide to live with a partner may also be more likely to divorce if they are unhappy with the relationship after taking vows, since they may have less conservative views of marriage. Let me be clear, living together is not marriage – nor is it a step toward marriage. If you find yourself cohabitating with your mate, please know that you can hit the restart button and do it God's way. His grace is sufficient for you, and His strength is made perfect in weakness. Moving forward, you can decide to remain chaste. Make a radical decision if you are living together that you or your fiancé will move in with a friend or family member until the wedding day. I know that's easier said than done, but it's only temporary. At the same time, if the relationship isn't moving in the direction of marriage, you need to reconsider it.

God promises to provide what you need when we are in right standing with Him. You will be amazed at the blessings and provisions you position yourself for when you align yourself with God's design. I promise you, your obedience will be worth it! I cannot say this enough: you are to be on a road to becoming a WIFE, not a fiancé and certainly not a live-in girlfriend.

Some will tell you that money and paying for the wedding is the reason why they haven't gotten married yet. Weddings are magical and beautiful. It is a time when friends and family can share in the celebration of love between a man and woman. I highly encourage everyone who can afford it to have one. However, the only funds involved in getting married is the cost of a marriage license, which, in most states, is under $100. A wedding is optional. Couples can get married in front of a minister and celebrate sometime later with a reception. I understand it's the norm to have a wedding celebration with all the festivities, but, contrary to popular belief, it is optional.

Studies have shown that couples who spend less on their wedding tend to stay married longer. And couples who decide to have an expensive wedding tend to bring the stress from the debt of the wedding into the relationship. Over time, this could cause the demise of the marriage.[3]

marital prep vs. wedding prep

Preparing for the wedding and preparing for marriage are not the same. The primary focus for the wedding is on the right dress, the best DJ, the prettiest cake and most picturesque venue. Some women began planning their wedding when they were little girls as they anticipated marrying their Prince Charming. Now, we even have Pinterest to help us catalog those dreams.

The wedding will take months to plan and only involve a few hours of celebrating with family and friends. The marriage will be years of living together as husband and wife, resolving conflicts, wading through communication challenges, living through the seasons of life—all the while raising a family, making a living, and leaving a legacy. Why would you invest more preparation into being a bride than becoming a wife?

Weddings are a billion-dollar industry. Women will stop at nothing to have the wedding of their dreams and live out their Pinterest boards. Countless hours are spent on wedding plans and ceremonies, but sadly, only a fraction of the time and money is spent on premarital preparation.

So, what does marital prep look like? I'm glad you asked. First, you must become mature, loving, unselfish, forgiving, and a secure individual with a clear understanding of your expectations, needs, likes, dislikes, and requirements. Can you communicate them effectively and honestly determine how well another person is suited to complement those prerequisites?

The bottom-line is to work on yourself *before* you marry to ensure you are ready to assume the responsibilities of marriage. Be certain you can make and accept decisions that are in the best interests of your new family, rather than just yourself. You must ask yourself the hard questions. Are you sufficiently mature enough to forgive? Are you able to leave the past in the past? Can I effectively communicate when a problem arises and work through it to a viable solution?

Be a confident, secure, and well-adjusted individual, who is truly prepared to share their life with someone else, yet who doesn't *need* a relationship to feel valuable. I understand this isn't as fun and exciting as planning a wedding. You must understand, however, that it is critical to the success and longevity of your marriage.

You must be able to talk about a number of things with your potential husband. No topic should be off-limits or avoided. Have you discussed expectations, past experiences, life choices, finances, having children, sex, hurts, etc.? Marital prep is the time to talk about it all. Communication is key, and having clear direction on these matters is important when there are no problems to resolve. Are you both aware of the other's tendencies, likes, dislikes and goals? There should be adequate discussion of these matters in comparison to the amount of time and effort placed on the details of the wedding. Instead of only picking out the colors and flowers for your big day, you should take valuable time to identify and express the way you both feel comfortable talking to one another.

As you prepare for married life, you should read books on marriage and attend marriage conferences. You should find a marriage mentor couple, a seasoned married couple who can become a sounding board and a safe place to explore questions about marriage. If you invest time and attention into preparing for the journey of becoming one and do the work, you will be well on your way to increased marital success.

It is very important that couples take the necessary steps, including premarital counseling, which we will talk about later. Some may figure it will all work itself out. This couldn't be further from the truth. In the corporate world, there is an adage that says, "Proper planning prevents poor performance." These steps are not just necessary before you get married, they are actually what you must do during the tenure of your marriage if you want it to thrive and not just survive.

what I wish I knew before getting married

If asked, many women can tell you something they wish they knew before they got married. There would be an array of answers. Everyone has something they wish they could have taken into consideration or been more aware of before getting married.

What I have discovered from women who have been married for 4 years or 40 years is they mostly wish they really knew that part of the work to make the marriage successful was about themselves. What I'm asking you to do to become wife ready includes your personal relationship with the Lord. Does your relationship with Him supersede all others? Is He truly first in your life? Is He your Lord and Savior? Have you truly submitted your life and everything that pertains to it to Christ?

Many women feel that, if they had known more about who they are in Christ before they began looking for a mate, their marriage would be better off. To get to the work of marriage, there's some 'work' you need to do on yourself beforehand. You must pray and ask God to show you yourself and what changes need to happen. Be intentional in spending time with Him in prayer every day and studying His Word.

I took a poll and asked several women what they wish they knew. While many of them shared valuable insights, one woman's answer stood out to me.

I have seen this repeated in so many relationships, only to be discovered after much heartache. This is what she shared:

"What I wish someone told me or taught me about marriage is... how to become a whole person. I've found out that, when two broken people come together, the results are a broken marriage. I wish I was taught to know how to be a woman of God and choose the man God has for me according to His Word. Don't get me wrong, I have no regrets, I love my husband, but how much better would our relationship be if we both followed Christ, and knew who we were in Him, *before* we were married?

Folks don't think about that before marriage—that it's literally all about Jesus. I knew Him, or knew of Him, growing up in a Christian home, but as far as knowing Him enough to make the right decision on a man—not close enough. The heartache I still go through at times tells the tale of a marriage that can only be strengthened and recovered by God. I wish someone had sat me down and told me that I should know who I am in Christ first and seek His Word to find what to look for in a man, and make sure that man has done the same thing. I wish I had known that I should court and date with a purpose and not give my heart away, and awaken love before it's time."

Listen to the heart of this woman, and take her advice before you give your heart away. While she loves her husband, she understands her marriage would be vastly different had she taken the time to passionately and patiently pursue God's purpose for her life and relationship. Her thoughts about what she wishes she'd known will be addressed in the next chapter.

Emotional wholeness and knowing yourself are the foundation on which your marriage must be built. It's not optional if you want your marriage to thrive, not just survive. It is a vital necessity. There is no way around it. Because "when"—not "if"—the storms come, your foundation is what will sustain your relationship.

What have you built your relationship on? Will it be sex, addictions, or the heritage of divorce in your bloodline? Or will it be your faith in the Word of God that anchors you? So many couples are calling it quits because of "irreconcilable differences," but in Christ there aren't any differences which cannot be reconciled. You need a Christ-centered marriage.

practical steps to becoming wife ready

1. Knowledge is power. Read as many books beforehand about the institution of a Christian marriage.

2. Do a self-examination to determine if you are more in love with the idea of marriage than the responsibility of it.

3. Ask women in your inner circle what they wished someone told them about marriage. Glean from it.

who are you?

2

who are you?

Identity is everything! You are a daughter of the King!
You are fearfully and wonderfully made. When God
created you, He created a masterpiece. You were made
in the image of God, and your Heavenly Father is
crazy about you!

Your identity must be rooted in Christ and
the finished work on the cross. You cannot look for it
anywhere else or in anyone else. God created you with
a portion of your soul that only He can fill. Nothing or
no one will ever be able to fill it. No career, no ministry,
no man, no child, and no amount of money can fill that

place in your life or complete you. If you attempt to fill that longing with anything other than God, you will be in a repetitive cycle of dissatisfaction and emptiness. You can attempt to fill it by exterior means, but it will never truly satisfy the God-size longing in your soul.

Before becoming a wife, you must know who you are in Him (God) so you can be what you need to be to him (your husband). A foundation in the Word, prayer, and daily devotions are vital for this to occur. Your relationship with the Lord has to supersede all others. You must renew your mind to the truths of God's Word concerning your identity.

One of my favorite passages is 2 Peter 1:2-3 (NASB), "Grace and peace be multiplied to you in the knowledge of God and of Jesus our Lord, seeing that His divine power has granted to us everything pertaining to life and godliness, through the true knowledge of Him who called us by His own glory and excellence." Everything you need to be a great wife is already in you through the finished work of Jesus. Any direction, instruction, or wisdom can be found in God's Word. You must develop it, and you do that by aligning yourself with what the Word says about marriage and being a wife.

It's not only critical to know your identity in Christ, but you need to also know where you fit into the Kingdom. You have a call on your life. You were created on purpose, with a purpose, and for a purpose. You have a Kingdom assignment and a destiny to fulfill. Do you know what that is? You will have to give an account for what God asked you to do. There is more to life than earning an income, having a family, growing old, and going to be with Jesus. We are supposed to make a difference in this world as we pass through it with the purpose God has assigned us.

Jeremiah 1:5 (NASB) says, "Before I formed you in the womb, I knew you, and before you were born, I consecrated you." What has God called you to do? What is your purpose? What empowers and fulfills you? What are you passionate about, and what comes naturally for you? Your purpose was placed in you before you were born. It's not something you decide; it is to be discovered.

If you don't know who you are, how will you know what kind of mate you need for you to be all that God has called you to be? You need to know that this man will fit into the continuity of who you are and what God has called you to do.

Choosing a life partner is a very important decision that will profoundly impact the rest of your life. Again, it is the second most important decision you will ever make with Jesus being the first. It's not something to enter into lightly. Not knowing who you are and being tired of being alone will cause you to settle just for the sake of being married, and it's not worth it. It is not God's intended purpose for your life or for your marriage.

Speaking of being alone, you can be alone and not necessarily lonely. It *is* possible to be single and not lonely just as it is also possible to be married and lonely. That's why marriage is not the antidote for loneliness. Ask someone who has been married for some time.

Knowing who you are will keep you from falling into the trap of marrying someone just because you are lonely. Being alone is simply *electing* to be by yourself. Lonely people often feel hollow and empty inside and attempt to fill that void with various means.

Loneliness makes you feel emotionally and socially disconnected from those around you. Recent statistics indicate more than 60% of lonely people are married.[4] When married couples no longer share their deepest feelings, thoughts, and experiences with one another, it can leave them feeling disconnected and alone over time.

We all experience seasons of feeling lonely. Marriage will not dispel this feeling. Trying to rid yourself of the experience of loneliness cannot be the reason you seek marriage. You may be living the age old saying of "always the bridesmaid and never the bride." You may have been single much longer than you ever anticipated or preferred to be. Being by yourself may have become stale and monotonous. Anyone who has been there knows loneliness gets stifling week after week, year after year, holiday after holiday. However, please do not allow your temporary circumstance to cause you to marry a man who isn't ready or mature enough to handle the responsibilities of marriage.

know your worth

I had a young couple who began the process of premarital counseling with me. By the time they were slated to meet and unpack their premarital assessment, the young lady had broken up with the guy and no longer desired to get married to him. He asked me to talk to his fiancé in hopes she would meet with me. He insisted I call her to ask if she would agree to at least one meeting. His goal was for me to talk her into reconciling with him. I explained to the young man my belief that it wouldn't do any good for me to talk with her, because she had to come to that decision on her own. He was persistent with her and persuasive, and she eventually conceded to one session.

When I met with them, she shared her reason for ending the relationship. She told me she did not appreciate the way he treated her. She said she deserved more than he was willing to give. She had given him multiple chances in various circumstances of their relationship. However, this time, he had been involved in some inappropriate behavior with other women that surfaced on social media. The reason she was letting him go was because she said he needed to get his act together before he tried to enter into a lasting relationship with anyone. She went on to say that she refused to devalue who she was or be second place, and was not willing to invest any more time in the relationship. More importantly, she wanted to focus on her relationship with the Lord and suggested that he do the same.

As I sat there listening, I smiled and cheered inwardly. I actually wanted to jump up and down, chest bump and high-five her! This young lady is every premarital counselor's and mentor's dream. She knew who she was and wasn't willing to settle for anything for the sake of being in a relationship. She didn't make excuses for him. She clearly made the break up about herself, focusing on what she needed and wanted in a relationship, not about him and his issues. That, my dear, should always be the case. It's about what *you* want and need—not his shortcomings. You cannot change him, undo his mistakes, or make up for his shortcomings.

When you know your own worth and value, you will refuse to allow a man to disrespect you and then make excuses for his behavior. Any time you break up with someone because you realize what you see in them is not what you want, it must be about you and not them. See it as a blessing when they show you who they really are. However, if you continue in a relationship where you don't feel valued and respected, you must stop asking why they keep doing what they're doing and ask yourself why you keep allowing it. Pause and think about that!

Does this sound like you? Are you devaluing who you are for the sake of being with someone? Do you lack the courage to end the relationship like this young lady did? Do you feel as if you have invested too much time into the relationship to just walk away? If so, please understand that several years of history aren't worth sacrificing a lifetime of destiny. It doesn't matter how much time you have invested in it. That pales in comparison to spending the rest of your life in an unhealthy relationship. Why settle for subpar? Ask yourself what is broken inside of you that allows yourself to be treated that way.

The concept you have of yourself is what attracts the caliber of people in your life. Mature men are attracted to confident women who know who they are. The air you have about yourself isn't arrogance; it is confidence. Arrogance is an attitude of superiority manifested in an overbearing manner. Confidence is the quality or state of being certain. Know your worth! Your future depends on it.

counterfeit before the real

If something is counterfeit, it has the intention to deceive or defraud. Any time we are with someone who is not meant to be our spouse, nothing good will come of it. While there may be good moments, those moments will not make your life better. They may cause emotional pain that takes months and even years to process and overcome. Recreational dating may be fun. However, if you are looking for a long-term relationship that leads to marriage, dating for fun will not yield that result.

The counterfeit is a great replica of the real. It seems that usually the counterfeit is what shows up before your soulmate does. The enemy seems to always be willing to offer you less than best. You don't have to date the counterfeit; you just need to be able to discern him. You do that by paying attention to that tug in your heart that something isn't quite right, to the red flags that are staring you in the face, and/or the fact you are, in moments of truest honesty with yourself, still looking for something more.

Just because the phone isn't ringing off the hook with potential candidates doesn't mean you have to settle for the first thing that comes along. Knowing who you are and being sensitive to the voice of the Holy Spirit is vital so you don't fall for the counterfeit. The more time you spend with the Lord, the better you will know His voice.

I personally experienced this. It happened to me. I dated the counterfeit, thinking he was "the one" for me. I had an idea of what I wanted in a husband, but being so young, I didn't know who I was. As a 19-year-old, there is no way you know who you are or what you need. You just haven't reached that level of maturity yet.

When God gets ready to bless you with a mate, some say there will be a glow about you, and men in general will see it. You may be approached by a number of them in a short period of time. It will be like fanning flies. During this time, your discernment is critical so you don't become involved with someone out of desperation or flattery. I understand you tire of being alone and desire companionship. We were made for relationships. What price, though, are you willing to pay to become emotionally and romantically involved with someone just for the sake of not being by yourself? The price is too high, and there is too much at stake to settle for anything less than what God has planned for your life and who He intends you to share that life with.

After not dating for two years, two different guys pursued me within a few weeks of each other. Naturally, I chose the one that looked like what I had on paper. That was a no brainer. Right? Wrong! Having a list of what you want isn't good enough. He can't just look good on paper. You have to know in your heart that he is the one for you. That begins first and foremost when you know who you are. If there is no connection or chemistry, don't overlook that. You can't go on what anyone thinks about how good you look together or how they perceive your compatibility for each other to be. You have to know for yourself! You will be the one building a life with him, not them.

The guy I chose asked for my number and shortly thereafter we began dating. It didn't take long to realize he wasn't ready for a commitment. He made every excuse in the book of why we should take our time. Time? I had plenty of time to think about what I wanted in a mate. I didn't need any more time. However, I overlooked his non-committal attitude and behavior and kept pursuing the chemistry and connection we had. He was evidently not ready for a relationship with me, and I didn't want to accept that. I just knew there was no way I had waited so long and now he would not be my mate. I was willing to wait for him to change his mind about how fast or slow the relationship was progressing. That was a huge red flag, but I put blinders on and refused to accept the obvious.

Have you made a similar decision in a relationship? I made excuses for his behavior and allowed myself to be deeply hurt by his lack of readiness. It wasn't his fault that I got hurt. It was my fault for allowing him to treat me the way he did. I didn't value myself and attracted someone in my life who didn't value me either. You attract who you are.

This indecisiveness went on for months. The longer I allowed him to manipulate my emotions, the harder it became. I had to come to the end of myself in order to move on with my life. He never came around and fully committed to anything. I finally realized my worth and value, after experiencing a trip to the doctor for a tightness in my chest because of severe stress and losing 15 lbs. in three weeks. A clean break was necessary for my sanity's sake and emotional wellbeing. I needed time to heal.

As bad as I wanted to be in a relationship, this guy wasn't "the one" for me. I was marriage-minded, and that was the furthest thing from his mind. While I was trying to force fit his non-committal and ambiguous behavior, the right one couldn't get to me, because I was tied up with the wrong one. Let that speak to you. If you know the guy you are with isn't right for you, why are you still hanging on? Respect yourself enough to walk away from a relationship that no longer works for you. You deserve better. A few weeks later, "my guy" walked into my life and shortly thereafter, in the plan and timing of God, we were on track to get married.

How many of you can identify with my story? Love does not hurt. Love shouldn't cause exhaustion and stress you out. Love won't leave you drained, distraught, or depressed. Yet, I was experiencing all of these. Sometimes on the same day! Love is a friend, protector, and healer. How could I believe that my future spouse was someone who perpetually hurt me? Marriage takes commitment and trust, and my first choice and I didn't have either. It's critical to not allow your desperation to be in a relationship overrule your discernment of it not being right. Trying to force fit a situation now will only lead to chaos later.

Single ladies, take your time in moving forward with a man who you believe could be "the one" God has chosen for you. While there is no "perfect will" versus "permissible will" when it comes down to God's will and a mate for your life, there is someone who is more suitable for you. Genesis 2:18 (NASB) says, "Then the LORD God said, "It is not good for the man

33

to be alone; I will make him a helper suitable for him."
That's why we must partner with God to discover who
that is, because your marriage has a purpose.

On the other hand, God has given each one of
us a free will, and we have more control over our lives
than He does. Shocking, huh? Well, we do. He gave us
dominion in the garden when He created mankind. He
cannot and will not override our free will. So choose
to align your choice to who God has chosen for you.
If your heart's desire is truly to honor Him in all that
you do, He will let you know if you're about to make
a mistake. Just don't override that nudge in your heart.
He always knows what's best for us.

you are the prize

Have you lowered your standards according to what is
available to you based on your feelings and emotions
about yourself rather than what the Word of God says
about you? Are you afraid to let go of what you have for
fear you'll never get what you desire? Do you know the
guy you are with is not right for you, but you're settling
because you don't want to be alone? What does your
gut tell you? Have others in your circle picked up on
some of the same things you have identified that aren't
quite right with this guy, but you refuse to acknowledge
them? Have you turned and looked the other way?

You don't have to settle just for the sake of being in a relationship. You are the upgrade! You are the prize! Always remember that! You are the one who connects your man to the favor of God. Proverbs 18:22 (NASB) says, "He who finds a wife finds a good thing and obtains favor from the Lord." The favor of God in a man's life is connected to his obedience and commitment to God. Certain blessings are released in his life when he marries the woman who is suitable for him.

The first step in attracting someone who is suitable for you is to see the value in who you are. You have greatness in you, and you have to believe that! You have to understand your worth and love yourself before you love anyone else. You can't give someone something you don't have. Do you care about others more than you do yourself? How do you see yourself? Do you love who you are just as you are? How confident are you about who God created you to be? Many women marry the wrong man or fail in their marriages because they do not place a high enough value on themselves.

The more you love yourself, the less foolishness you will tolerate. You won't let men run roughshod over your emotions. You won't put up with their bad behaviors just for the sake of being with someone. You won't beg them to see your worth. If they can't see what's right in front of them, they don't deserve you.

It is not selfish to love yourself; that's a misconception that couldn't be further from the truth. It's like the oxygen mask theory of self-care. Most of us have been on an airplane and heard the safety warning before the flight that, if the pressurization should fail, you must put on your own oxygen mask before trying to help others. The same theory can be applied to life. How can you love someone unless you love yourself first?

Has your life been on hold waiting for you to live it to the fullest, because you are waiting to get married? Singleness should not be a waiting room for marriage. You must be actively living your life, not passively waiting for a man.

practical steps to discovering who you are

1. Renew your mind daily to what God says in His Word about you.

2. Choose to base your identity on God's love for you rather than on what others think of you.

3. Speak to yourself in the mirror daily about how fearfully and wonderfully made you are. If you don't believe it, who else will?

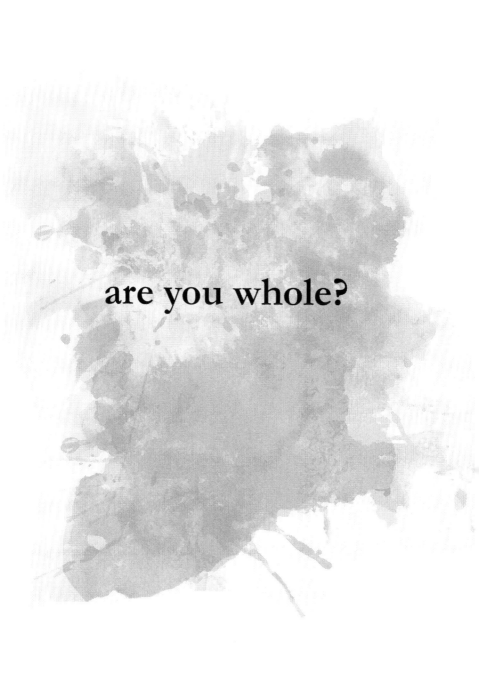

are you whole?

3

are you whole?

Your emotional wellbeing will play a huge role in your marriage. It is better that you don't get married before you experience an inner healing. In his book, *Date or Soul Mate?*, Dr. Neil Clark Warren states that, in 75-80% of all marriages that eventually end in divorce or separation, at least one of the marriage partners suffers from an emotional health deficiency. It is vital to become emotionally whole before committing to a long-term relationship.[5]

Circumstances occur in one's life that can cause us to be broken in many ways. If we aren't careful, we unconsciously try to fill that brokenness with a relationship. If you choose your mate in a state of brokenness, all it will do is perpetuate brokenness.

You also need to address any daddy issues. Was your father absent in your life? Was he physically present but emotionally unavailable? Did he physically, emotionally, or sexually abuse you?

The trauma of your past will severely impact your relationship with your husband and children if you are not emotionally healed. What unresolved conflict do you or your partner have? What deep-seated wound do you carry that has not healed? It doesn't matter how long ago the offense happened; if it hasn't been confronted, acknowledged, or processed, it's still there. When we bury our issues, we bury them alive. They don't die but, rather, come out in other ways in our behavior and body language—oftentimes over the course of your entire life—if they're not dealt with. We can act as if nothing ever happened and live in denial of the pain. The issue will control us if we don't take control of it.

If you are dealing with a lack of trust, bitterness, or anger, it is important that you identify the root cause. Was it the divorce, rejection, or abandonment of your own parents? Were you physically, mentally, sexually, or verbally abused by someone? The people closest to you will bear the brunt of your pain if you are not emotionally healed. You will hurt the person you love, with no explanation and no way to help them heal after you hurt them.

Have you heard the saying, "Hurt people, hurt people?" It's more than just a quaint saying; it is a profound truth. From their place of pain, hurting people act out in ways that hurt others.

You must deal with the brokenness and unresolved issues in your life. If not, you will oftentimes find yourself repeating a cycle of frustration and dysfunction that, in turn, limits and can even destroy intimacy. Intimacy is unhindered access and emotional closeness. True love cannot flow through your heart when it is clogged with fear, pain, and hurt.

Too often, the pain is so unbearable we choose to keep it suppressed. Suppressing emotions come in the form of not talking about them to numbing them with various addictions.

How do you know if healing has occurred? When you can talk about the issue and not be affected by it, and when you have forgiven your offender. It's when you can share what you have been through to help someone else get through what they are going through. It's when you don't want revenge. Under the guidance and safety of a biblical counselor, you can peel back the layers, expose the root of your pain, and navigate your way through the terrain of getting healed.

The demise of many marriages is attributed to irreconcilable differences. At the core of those differences are money fights and money challenges, infidelity, and addictions, including, but not limited to drugs, food, shopping, alcohol, and pornography. Some of these addictions are a byproduct of a deeper issue of unprocessed pain, the individual's lack of emotional healing, and the void they are trying to fill. Once healing has occurred in these areas, you will be well on your way to freedom.

parental impact

Our parents have a profound impact in our lives in both positive and negative ways. Children expect their parents to nurture, support, protect, and affirm them. Unfortunately, some adults are unable to properly fulfill the needs of their children due to the lack in their own lives. They simply can't give what they don't have.

The decisions they made for us in our formative and adolescent years will impact us in adulthood. If your parents have unresolved hurts, hardships, and issues from their past, you will bear the brunt of it. What wasn't transformed in them is transferred to you. If they are emotionally healthy, you will benefit greatly. Reading this book may put some things in perspective for you to realize and better understand what has been occurring and going on throughout your own life as it pertains to relationships.

How did your childhood and the way you were parented affect your relationships? Pause and think about that. A large part of who you are stems from how you were raised, as well as what you observed and were exposed to growing up.

One of the first things I do with couples who come to me for premarital counseling is dig into their past by asking a series of questions about their relationship with their parents or stepparents. The conditions of the home environment, including the quality of their parents' marriage and parent-child interactions, show me the influence of their choices as an adult.

What I have discovered is that a lot of what adults are dealing with is directly linked to their childhood. At some point, something was said or done that impacted them deeply and totally altered their life as they once saw and experienced it. When the trauma of abuse (whether physical, mental, or sexual), abandonment, or rejection occurs, the innocence of that child is stolen, and their life is emotionally scarred. While the pain runs deep from that offense against you, take heart! If you allow the power of the Holy Spirit in, He can heal, restore, and make you whole again. You don't have to live your entire life in pain. That's why Jesus came!

Have you been personally impacted by the pain of one or both of your parents? Looking back to your early years, have you been able to "connect the dots" to something that happened in your parents' lives that you are now dealing with in your own life? It is imperative that you take the necessary steps to overcome what has happened. You may not get the answers you desire from either parent about why and how they were hurt. You may or may not be able to facilitate a level of healing and help for them. However, you can begin your own personal journey toward healing, health, and wholeness.

If you go into marriage with a moderate degree of unresolved issues with your parents, at times you might find yourself leaning on your partner to meet needs that weren't met when you were growing up. What we didn't receive from our parents in terms of affection, support, and direction, we often expect from other relationships in adulthood. This may compel us to look for healing from childhood hurts from others as well. The Holy Spirit is the only One who can heal and eradicate any emotional deficiencies from our past.

On the other hand, the impact our parents have over how we navigate life may not all be negative. In fact, it all may play out in how we view marriage or men in a positive way. You witnessed the love, affection, and respect modeled by your parents' relationship. They may have a Christ-centered marriage, which is what you aspire to have. You know they've had challenges along the way, but they chose to work through them and their love has grown stronger and deeper for one another over the years. They anticipate each other's needs and literally complete one another's sentences. They are indeed best friends and lovers.

Either way, we need to realize that how we grew up, what we were exposed to, what was expected of us, and how our world was shaped as children will have a direct impact on our interactions with people as adults. This will also be the case for your spouse. He has his own set of ideologies and philosophies based on his life experiences. You two will need to talk through all of this… find the commonalities, and agree on what your way of life as a married couple is and how your marriage relationship will look.

My husband and I benefited greatly from the Christ-centered homes we were reared in. My parents raised my siblings and me with the Word of God being the authority on which we lived our lives. My husband's mother, though a single parent, raised him and his sisters with the same foundation. It paid off in tremendous ways by allowing both of us to bring this foundation of faith to build our marriage upon.

My parents' marriage represents how Christ loves the church. They are still together today after 55 years. I learned how to be a godly wife by watching my mom; I knew what I wanted in a husband by observing my father and the way he treated her. Even being raised the way I was, I still had the responsibility to mature in the things of God as an adult.

Recently, one of my clients, a married woman, asked to meet with me. She began to share some things that were happening with her husband and needed some guidance. Her husband's father left his family when he was a young boy. He was very devastated by the abandonment he experienced as a youth, and it took him years to process the fact that his father was no longer around. Dealing with her own pain, hurt, and loss, unfortunately his mother never initiated the healing process by having her son deal with his pain under the guidance of a counselor or pastor.

Throughout his married life, the pocket of pain he never worked through would rear its head in the form of fear, insecurity, and anger. He suffered tremendously with his self-concept and inadequacies of being a man—not having had the role of father and husband modeled for him. There was an angry undercurrent which surfaced when his manhood was challenged, which stemmed from these insecurities. For some men, it is easier to become angry than deal with the emotions fueling the anger.

Due to his lack and inability to process his emotions, he often stonewalled his wife by shutting her out for days at a time. She felt and had to deal with the brunt of his unaddressed and unhealed pain without always understanding its source. He didn't shut down intentionally to hurt her. His actions and reactions were coming from a pocket of pain he carried from childhood into adulthood. Had this young man married his wife in a state of emotional wholeness, they may not have encountered certain issues in their relationship.

Are you with a man who has similar tendencies? Are there certain conversations that trigger his anger? Is he controlling? Does he get angry about honest questions? Does he talk to you like you're his daughter instead of his partner? Some fatherless sons have a tendency to "father" their wives by the way they speak to them and desire to control their actions. I believe they are trying to prove something to themselves, having not been fathered themselves.

This could all be a sign that he's trying to convince himself that he can handle manhood when actually he's just a scared little guy inside. His controlling behavior could stem from the fact that he didn't have a relationship with his father and, also out of fear of losing you.

Don't gloss over this! Before the "I do's," you must have the hard conversations required to get to the crux of the matter that fuels this behavior. If you don't, you will bump up against this in your marriage until it is healed.

inner vows

To have a successful marriage, you cannot carry emotional baggage from one relationship to another. If you have been hurt in a past relationship and go into the next one guarding your heart with an inner vow, your relationship is already in trouble before it begins.

An inner vow is a self-promise related to a difficult circumstance. We create inner vows to comfort ourselves. The new guy in your life won't have all of your heart, because you are protecting a part of it. With an inner vow, your current guy will pay for what the old one (or even your parents) did. True intimacy cannot develop if you don't disengage from what you are holding on to, become vulnerable, and renounce those inner vows.

Being disengaged is a barrier to intimacy, and your relationship will seem as if it keeps hitting a brick wall. Barriers to intimacy are those things that block or somehow prevent intimacy from occurring in our marriage relationship. They make it difficult to understand or connect with your spouse and can lead to a breakdown in the relationship.

If you have been wounded on the battlefield of love, marriage won't heal it. You must take the necessary steps towards inner healing with the help of the Holy Spirit in order to be made whole again. Emotional healing is a process, one that you cannot do in your own strength. A very powerful resource that I recommend to my clients is the 21 Day Inner Healing Journey by Jimmy Evans of MarriageToday.[6] This online devotional has helped many become healed and reclaim their lives, learning to live abundantly as Jesus died for them to do.

Medical personnel are trained to treat wounds. They have taken the necessary classes and obtained information on how to care for and treat their patients.

The same applies to emotional trauma. Only the help of someone who has been trained to care for the soul and the impact of emotional devastation can help you process such pain. Seek the help of a faith-based counselor if you need to.

A couple came to me for premarital counseling. The guy had been verbally abused by his parents growing up. His heart was guarded because of the hurt he experienced for most of his life. As a result, his relationship was strained as a young adult. During our session, I noticed how guarded and non-conversational he was. Any attempt to have him open up failed as he sat quietly and offered "one word" answers to my questions. It was challenging to converse with him with these walls up and his guarded persona.

At one point in the counseling session, a recent incident with his fiancée's family surfaced. It left him feeling disrespected in front of her family, which triggered the deep-seated hurt he experienced from his parents. He admitted to me he had a hard time trusting people and was always reluctant to let anyone "in."

I lovingly shared my heart on how damaging this behavior can be. I explained how trust is the foundation on which relationships are built. Without it, no marriage will work.

I strongly suggested to this couple that they work through these challenges before they took a step further. As a youth, he made an inner vow to himself that he would not let anyone hurt or disrespect him as his parents did. I advised him that, if he wanted to be in an intimate relationship, he had to deal with the pain from his past.

I have a heart for people. I want them to walk in freedom and the abundant life Jesus died for them to have. I also realize that men respond better to other men. With that, I offered to have him speak with one of our pastors to begin his healing journey, and he agreed. It was vital that he make a commitment for the long haul to be healed.

After meeting with the pastor, we continued the premarital counseling. I was hopeful that healing for this young man was imminent. To my surprise, I received a text informing me his fiancée postponed the wedding. In instances like this, most couples find every reason to move forward and believe things will somehow work out in the end. This couple heeded my advice and decided to delay the wedding to work on the issues they were experiencing in their relationship. However, he later informed me that they had called the wedding off all together. Weddings don't heal the pain; confronting the truth and dealing with the issues involved does.

make peace with the past

One of the ingredients necessary for a happy marriage is to be certain to deal with issues in our past. The truth is the past isn't the past until it has been dealt with properly. The past can affect our today in a negative manner; therefore, it is still in the present. Every person has some kind of baggage. Common examples of baggage are past hurts that have never been healed, unforgiveness from a transgression that has occurred, generational sins and patterns from the wrong behaviors to which we were exposed, or quirks in our personalities that have never been fixed.

All of us are the sum total of our pasts. The good things in our past produce the good qualities in our lives today. The bad things in our pasts that we haven't dealt with create personality problems, emotional issues, relational difficulties, and, last but not least, marriage trouble.

When you begin dealing with your past, the first thing to do is to surrender to Jesus and ask the Holy Spirit to reveal to you anything or anyone in your past you need to deal with. He desires to heal you where you hurt. Ask Him to illuminate the areas in your heart you need to deal with and overcome. He will. He desires you to be whole.

The second critical issue is forgiveness. Without forgiveness, our hurts become festering wounds that never heal and cause our personalities to be malformed around them. The simple act of forgiveness can set you free from your past and free for your future faster than almost anything else you can do. You may be wondering if forgiveness requires you to be in relationship with your offender. It doesn't. Forgiveness does not require reconciliation. Forgiveness is for you. It frees you. True forgiveness is when you relinquish your right to get even, respond to evil with good, and repeat the process as long as necessary.

You cannot allow what has happened to you to control what is possible for you. Don't make your husband pay for the things the last man did. Don't let your past cost you your future or color it in ways outside of God's design for you.

In order to deal with your past, be willing to be blatantly honest with yourself. We have a tendency to see the flaws in our spouse or boyfriend and associate them with how messed up their family is and then somehow be blind to our own issues. We need to honestly look at some of our less than stellar qualities and ask this question: "Could I be this way because of something in my past I haven't dealt with?"

Finally, we must take responsibility for our own problems. An example is the issue of generational sins and patterns. As we realize our parents may have modeled a wrong behavior to us, we must forgive them and then repent to God for our own sins. If we live blaming our parents or others in our past for our problems, we will never be set free. All behavior is chosen. You cannot continue to blame your parents for the flaws in your character. The statute of limitations has run out on your childhood pain. It is time to take responsibility for your own behavior, choices, and attitude. Your marriage can only be as healthy as the least healthy person in it. Therefore, it is vital that you become emotionally healed before getting married.

practical steps to becoming wife ready

1. Make a list of everyone who hurt you. Forgive them, and release yourself from the hurt. Repeat as often as necessary.

2. Take the 21 Day Inner Healing Journey at 21dayjourney.com.

3. Pick your pain—the pain of remaining the same or the pain of change, which is temporary.

are you wife material?

4

are you wife material?

While listening to a sermon series entitled, Mr. and Mrs. Better Half, Pastor Steve Furtick stated, "Inside every man is a king and a kid, a prince and a punk. The one that you speak to is the one he will act like."

Men gravitate to the place where they are honored most. If you don't honor him, someone else will. Men need respect like they need air. It's innate. It's how they are wired to respond. The Bible even speaks of this in Ephesians 5:33. If you have experienced being stonewalled or shut down by your man, chances are he felt disrespected. Men are so hungry for respect;

they gravitate to wherever it comes from. You can't allow another female, be his mother or daughter, to out honor you when it comes to your man. The dynamics of those relationships are vastly different, but the praise they give him will still grab at his heart.

Your husband should be so confident of your respect and reverence for him he should never walk into a room, see you in a corner with your friends, and wonder if you're talking ill of him. His heart should so safely trust in you that the vibe he gets from other women is about how good he treats you. Any disagreements or issues you have need to be discussed with him in private, not with your friends or family members. If you can't resolve it among yourselves, seek wise counsel. Counseling isn't a sign of weakness; it is a sign of wisdom. Proverbs 12:15 (NASB) says, "The way of a fool is right in his own eyes, but a wise man is he who listens to counsel."

If you want to experience a life-giving, fulfilling marriage, it will come from a relationship with Jesus Christ. Everything you are and will need to be as a wife can be found in Him. There is no way your marriage can thrive without Christ at the center. After all, it was His idea.

Being a wife requires that you have the characteristics and mindset of a wife. Being married is not just a status, it is a condition of the heart. You can't be single-minded and be married. It's not about you. Proverbs 18:22 (NASB) says, "He who finds a wife finds a good thing, and obtains favor from the

Lord." You don't become a wife when you get married; you are already a wife when your husband finds you. A wedding doesn't make you a wife, it makes you married. A wife is not just a title—it's a responsibility.

So what does wife material look like? I'm not certain I personally care for that term, however it's a popular description in today's society and something women today are defining themselves by.

First, the wife ready woman should be in submission and obedience to Christ and should put Him before everything and everyone. He will then prepare you for the natural husband He has planned for your life.

Second, from a natural standpoint, who could better describe what wife material looks like than a man himself. I asked several men that very question and how they would know if a woman was wife ready. Many of the responses pointed back to you knowing who you are first in Christ and having your own relationship with the Lord without feeling as if your man will complete you. They also shared that you should understand you are a treasure that has worth and value and should refuse to be treated as less than such.

Effective communication and critical thinking skills were important subject matters as well. In addition, they wanted someone who is domesticated. It's difficult for someone who is a neat freak to live with a not-so tidy person. She should exemplify the fruit of the Spirit, be a partner not a dependent, and a best friend and recreational partner with whom they can have fun. The men indicated they want women who are true to themselves, who don't present a stylized ideal version of herself while dating, since the real woman will surface over the course of forever.

They want someone with a similar lifestyle and mindset. They want to look forward to coming home to someone with whom they can share the ups and downs of their day. Of course they wanted intimacy and fidelity. Similar hobbies are appreciated, as well as an appreciation and understanding of the need to do some things alone. These men didn't want a woman who forgets who she really is because she's married to him. Yes, you are Mrs. So & So, but that's not all you are. There is so much more depth to you than that.

They feel it is important for the health of your relationship that you and he are interdependent, not codependent. You exist as individuals, not just as a part of a coupled whole. A relationship is about two separate individuals coming together and complementing each other. It is not about completely giving up your own interests or desires for the other person or the relationship.

They want a willingness to sacrifice for one another because of the deep bond you share and a belief you will have each other's back even in difficult times. Spiritual, ethical, and moral values must be in alignment as well. This was also important to them since different values will make or break any relationship.

Lastly, the men felt a woman who is wife ready isn't nagging or overly vocal. She doesn't emasculate her man publicly or privately, nor is she always trying to challenge him with what she knows against what he doesn't.

All of this feedback I received was constructive and enlightening. However, one guy took it a step further by addressing men's marital readiness. I knew you were probably waiting to get to this, so let's talk about it.

He shared that a man needs to scrutinize himself first. He should be "husband worthy" and ready to accept the responsibilities of having a wife. Can he hold down a job, or is he always starting a new business venture? Is he pursuing realistic goals, or is he always chasing some new rainbow? What visions, dreams, and goals does he have for himself today and five years into the future? Does he know what his purpose in life is? Is he driven or complacent? What kind of father will he be? What kind of father did he have? By asking you to be his one and only, is he ready for the same? There needs to be some humility on his part. He needs to ask himself if he has dealt with any ego issues. He needs to choose you above all others when he asks the question. He also needs to understand, when you say "yes," you are choosing him above all others. He has to realize his hunt is over forever!

He needs to make a commitment to God that he will love you like Christ loves His church, wash you with the Word of God, and fulfill his covenant to be exclusively committed to you for the rest of his life. A good spouse is a gift from God and should be honored as such. Don't marry a man just for the sake of being married. Make certain, by being sensitive to the voice of the Lord, that he is God's choice for you.

selflessness and servanthood

The heartbeat of marriage requires selflessness, servanthood, and submission. If these are something you struggle with and aren't willing to change, marriage may not be for you. You must die to yourself when you get married. It's not as if you don't have needs, but your needs, in general, must be met inside the whole. It won't be about you all the time. Marriage is hard on people who are selfish and only think of themselves or think of themselves first all the time without any consideration of others.

If you have been single and living on your own for many years, being "others-conscious" will be a challenge for you, but it's not your fault. You should be proud of your independence. Having the means to live on your own and take care of yourself is a blessing. Living alone does not require you to think about anyone other than yourself. Single people settle into a pattern of living their lives exclusively, where common gestures of courtesy never cross their minds.

If you live alone, you don't have the pressure of keeping things neat, clean, and tidy at all times. It may not bother you to live with dirty dishes in the sink and discarded clothes on the floor. For some, you can't function with a home that's cluttered and in disarray. However, if you are a bit more relaxed in this area, now is the time to become more conscious of your living environment. Your man needs domestic support, a safe and clean haven to come home to. I don't believe the wife should bear all of the responsibility to maintain the cleanliness of the home. It is a joint effort. I do believe, however, that it is the woman's role to "manage the house" and "create the home."

Being wife ready and wife material requires self-discipline on your part. You must learn to think about someone other than yourself and now is a good time to begin. Start making a conscious effort to become accountable to someone else. Ask one of your girlfriends if you can text her twice a week and let her know when you get home in the evening. This will put you in the habit of letting someone know where you are and that are you are okay.

Your marriage will benefit greatly if you learn to give of yourself in the relationships you have with those around you. If you have a parent or relative nearby, ask if you can grab something from the store for them when you go for yourself. Invite some girlfriends over for a Saturday brunch occasionally and serve them. To be cost effective, it can be a potluck from time to time. However, the key is the experience—the preparation it takes to host and serve.

When you cook dinner, put some away in a freezer to give away to a friend or family member. This will provide you with constructive feedback about your meals and also the joy of cooking for someone else and learning how to cook in a larger quantity. If you don't know how to cook, now is the time to learn. You don't have to be a gourmet chef, but you need to know how to make something. Eating out will run its course at some point and add up financially. Uber Eats should not be a way of life.

These small gestures will put you on your way and mentally prepare you for being others-conscious. A paradigm shift has to be made, because in a marriage life is no longer about "me" but "we".

Marriage is all about servanthood. Jimmy Evans of MarriageToday states, "The greatest marriage is two servants in love; the worst marriage is two masters in love."[7] Paul talks about this very thing in Philippians 2:3-4 (NASB) when he says, "Do nothing from selfishness or empty conceit, but with humility of mind regard one another as more important than yourselves, do not merely look out for your own personal interests but also for the interests of others."

Why is this element so essential to the success of marriage? Our role model is Jesus Christ, who is the heart of servanthood. Serving isn't about being used. It is about choosing to give. Servants, like Jesus, willingly suspend their rights, privileges, time, and agendas to meet their spouse's needs. They choose to follow the example of Jesus by making a deliberate decision to serve. Start working on your serve or servitude.

single again

The dissolution of a marriage is very difficult. Life after divorce is challenging at best and can be truly overwhelming. You may feel lost, cheated, angry, embarrassed, and even guilty. It's an emotional roller coaster ride with an array of emotions that will take time to heal and process.

As a divorced woman, you may have picked up this book to read wondering what you could have done differently. Was I really wife ready when I got married? You may have asked yourself, "Did I put on blinders when I saw red flags?" "How did I attract this into my life?" "Was I so desperate to be married, I settled for less?" The concept you have of yourself is what attracts the caliber of people into your life.

You knew you couldn't change him but thought perhaps you could influence him to change. You believe in love and loved being married, but now you're picking up the pieces of your broken heart and are wondering, "Where do I go from here?"

Let me encourage you. Sometimes relationships just don't work out. Marriage is a very complex relationship, where two are becoming one. It requires both of you to say "I do." Unfortunately, though, it only takes one person to say, "I don't," and the relationship is over and headed for divorce. I personally do not believe that couples get married with the intent to divorce. They really believe their love will last a lifetime.

Marriage is a two-way street with both parties heading in the same direction. You cannot make anyone do anything they do not want to do. We each have a free will and are responsible for our own choices.

Perhaps your husband cheated on you; that was his choice. You may or may not have played a part in that decision, but ultimately, the choice was his. Did you use your body as a weapon against him? If you did, what does a wife expect when she starves her husband and he goes out for meals? Extramarital affairs typically don't happen overnight. Generally, something has gone awry long before a dissatisfied spouse begins to wander. Marriages don't get rocky; we throw rocks at marriage.

The question is, where do I go from here? I'm glad you asked. Everything begins with you, because you are the only one who can control you.

First, you must admit your part in the dissolution of your marriage. Let me interject here, too, that all marriages aren't dissolved because of infidelity. Whatever the case may be, in order to move on, you must take responsibility for what you may have contributed to the demise of the relationship, even if you feel it was only 2%.

Second, you must take time to heal. This is not an option. It is vital. You must take time to grieve, heal, recover, and learn the lessons. You should not consider dating for at least a year after your divorce is final. Avoid the temptation to manipulate this time frame by saying, "We were separated for six months before we filed…" or whatever other excuse you may find to shorten the time. Healing, especially emotional healing, takes time. It is wise to wait at least that long so you can evaluate your life, take inventory of who you are, change the things about yourself that you do not like, and discover exactly what you are looking for in a mate.

Third, reflect on any unrealistic expectations you had. There is nothing wrong with having expectations in a relationship. However, having unrealistic expectations can put stress on or ruin any relationship. An unrealistic expectation is expecting something out of the relationship that the other is either ignorant of, unwilling to provide, or simply unable to provide. It can be emotionally damaging for both partners and will lead to disappointment.

I want to expound a little more on unrealistic expectations. They can be a huge source of contention in marriage. This particular area was problematic in my own. I had expectations of how our finances would be managed. My dad handled the money in our home growing up, so that's what I expected of my husband. I did not want the responsibility of paying the bills. I wanted him to handle it. He'd say that I was better at it, but that didn't matter to me. I felt that he, as the man of the house and the leader of the home, should take the reins in making certain the finances were in order. That was immaturity on my part. I had an unrealistic expectation of him. My expectation matched my experience, but my experience was my past not our present. As previously stated, the experiences and expectations you bring into your marriage can and will work for or against you.

My husband wasn't "that guy" who could manage money well. That was no slight on him. He was a very hard worker and was not lazy by any means. I was simply better in this area than he was. He knew his limitations. That is what he'd tell me. Eventually, I stopped fighting it. We were able to come to a meeting of the minds and work together with me taking the financial lead.

The quicker you are able to identify what expectations are unrealistic in your marriage and come to an understanding of those things, the better it will be for the health and harmony of your relationship. You can't expect someone to give you something they don't have, or are incapable or unwilling to give.

a wise woman

An untamed tongue is a relationship killer. Our tongue has creative and destructive power. A woman's words are as strong as a man's fist. You can speak and build him up, or you can speak and break him in half. Sometimes a single word can make or break him. Take time to think about what you want to say, if you need to say it, and how you will say it. Someone else's heart is the recipient of your soft answer or your rapier sharp tongue.

You cannot say everything that comes to your mind; neither should you want to. A wise woman will know the difference. Understand that whatever comes out of your mouth cannot be retracted. Be wise in how and what you say. There will be times when you will need to be quiet in situations even when you are right. A wise man once told me, "Never miss an opportunity to shut up." Learning how to shut your mouth and filter your thoughts can prevent further damage from being done in your relationship.

Before making a comment, weigh your words by asking yourself, "Are my words needed? Would they be encouraging?" Proverbs 10:19 (NASB) says, "When words are many, transgression is not lacking, but whoever restrains his lips is prudent." I'm not suggesting that you be passive and a pushover. However, you can exercise wisdom when addressing sensitive issues.

I hate nothing more than a woman who demeans and emasculates her man. You can say anything to him at any time as long as your tone is right. Constantly riding and nitpicking him about small stuff can cause him to become defensive, shut down, and possibly stonewall you. Men don't want to be communicated with like they are boys. Regardless of how they may act at times, the appropriate reaction is never to demean them.

The wisdom you need to be a wife will not come naturally for you. Thank God for the provision He has provided for us in His Word. James 1:5 says we can ask God for wisdom; He will give it to us generously and not rebuke us for asking. The awesome thing about God is you can ask and ask again, as often as necessary, and He will always supply in abundance.

Instead of focusing on your mate's shortcomings, learn to recognize the wonderful things about him. Nobody wants to hear what's wrong all the time. Trust me, most men are fully aware of their faults and failures. Men need to be honored based on their position, not on their performance. A wise woman will choose to see the good and speak into that. Tell him how much you appreciate him and all that he does for you. Pray *for* him, not *about* him. Let him know you have his back no matter what. He may not tell you, but sometimes he's scared because of the weight and responsibility he has. Don't feed his fears! Build him up with faith. Let him know you trust and believe in him. Reassure him of God's love, faith, and trust in him.

You will not, I repeat, you will not always want to or feel like honoring him regardless of any position of headship, leadership, or anything else for that matter. However, sometimes you must push past how you feel and do what you need to do. Your feelings aren't in charge, you are.

Encouragement from you bears more weight than words from anyone else on the planet, so keep it that way. He married you. He is in love with you. He chose you. He ended his hunt with you.

A wise woman knows that she cannot change a man. However, she also knows she can inspire him to want to make changes. If you desire to see changes in your relationship, start with making them first, and watch him respond to the positive changes he sees in you.

practical steps to becoming wife ready

1. Discipline yourself to keep your house clean. Take a cooking class if you must.

2. Begin seeing, carrying, and envisioning yourself as a wife with all of the responsibilities that it entails.

3. Ask yourself daily what you can do to focus less on yourself.

how have you
prepared?

5

how have you prepared?

More couples than ever before want premarital education. Research has shown it is associated with higher levels of marital satisfaction and can better equip couples for marriage.[8] Those who do not participate in premarital preparation are more likely to see their problems as unsolvable. Being prepared is not about being perfect; it is about being wise and understanding the value of seeking wise counsel.

Investing in premarital counseling is the wisest decision any couple can make. Marriage is for grown ups. You have to prepare for the most important and complex relationship you will have in this life. This time of preparation will help immensely in the day to day of the relationship, while contributing exponentially to the longevity of your marriage. It will set proper expectations and demystify the unrealistic ones. When couples develop healthy habits early on in their relationship, they will have the tools to overcome future issues in their marriage.

There is a vast difference in preparing for the wedding and preparing for marriage. Preparing for the wedding doesn't automatically prepare you for marriage. Every year, millions of people get married, and millions get divorced. Every year billions of dollars and countless hours are spent on wedding plans and ceremonies. Sadly, only a fraction of the time and money is spent on premarital preparation. As a result, couples suffer from being unprepared for the marathon of marriage.

The wedding of your dreams can turn into a nightmare if you are unprepared. Premarital counseling is designed to go beneath the surface of a couple's relationship and focus on the foundation. As a certified SYMBIS (Saving Your Marriage Before It Starts) Facilitator,[9] I know firsthand how this tool will assist couples to delve deeply into how they can mesh their personalities, differences, and expectations.

In my opinion, premarital counseling is not something that should be optional. I appreciate pastors who are willing to make premarital counseling a pre-requisite to planning a wedding among their congregants. You cannot overthink or over-prepare for your future. This preparation time will give you a specific time and place to discuss any and everything pertinent to your future. Nothing and no subject is off limits. If you are engaged to someone who doesn't agree to premarital counseling, take that for what it is—a huge red flag! Do not gloss over it.

Personally, I would not marry anyone who is not willing to meet together with a qualified counselor to discuss important life issues before making such a life-changing commitment. There is no amount of premarital counseling that will help someone who never wanted to be married in the first place. If you are engaged because you placed pressure of any kind on your partner, you should think twice about your relationship. I don't suggest you call things off, however, I do suggest you pay attention to see if your relationship has shifted in any way.

In counseling, you can learn new tools on how to communicate with instant understanding and how to reduce and resolve conflict. Investing in your marriage beforehand will yield dividends throughout its duration. Unfortunately, it's the last thing on some couples' to-do list when, in fact, it should be the first.

In marriage, you must be prepared for anything, everything (and nothing) that can happen in and to your relationship at any given time. On your wedding day, you will make a vow "to have and to hold one another, for better or worse, richer or poorer, in sickness and in health, until death do you part" with no clue of what the future holds. It's one of the biggest leaps of faith you will ever take and will pay off in tremendous ways. Marriage can get better and better as the years go by.

When my husband and I married, we were great friends, and we were very much in love with each other. As storybook romantic as it sounds, I knew in my heart the day we met that we would be married one day. I can't offer you any logical reasoning for my conclusion, I just knew it in my spirit. We didn't have premarital counseling, as the church we attended didn't offer it, nor was it a part of our culture in the '80s. That began my quest for knowledge by asking other female friends about marriage.

Over the years, the seasons and stresses of everyday life threatened to destroy our relationship. I learned most of what I know about marriage in the school of hard knocks, because I was so young. However, no matter how difficult things became, **WE DECIDED** to work through them.

You will be faced with the same decision, time after time. I guarantee that it will be worth it every time you say, "Yes, let's work this out."

different economic philosophies

When I sit down with couples in a premarital counseling session, we talk in depth about finances. I ask if they have a Last Will and Testament, if they know one another's salaries, and have seen their credit reports? We discuss disclosure of any IRS debt, because that will not be reflected on their report. I ask if there is life insurance, retirement, and an emergency fund. If it's a blended family, are there any delinquent child support payments? These are the personal questions that must be answered before you say, "I do."

Money fights and money differences are at the top of the list of things couples fight about. It is imperative that you are both on the same page when it comes to finances, or you may end up in divorce court. If either of you have bad credit, it affects you both. If one is in a significant amount of debt, it becomes "our" debt." It's no longer "mine" and "yours," it becomes "ours." Are you ready to shoulder that debt? There is no such thing as "your student loans" when you get married. When you say, "I do", you acquire them no matter how much they are and to which organization they are owed.

Are you ready to live in and possibly raise your family in an apartment, because your credit is too bad to purchase a home? Better yet, how about renting a house and the landlord decides to sell, and you have to uproot your family before you are ready to? There are so many things to discuss beforehand.

There are important aspects of your family's finances that will need to be decided in advance. Even though we spoke about this in an earlier chapter, it bears repeating. Who will pay the bills? This role and responsibility needs to be taken on by whichever one of you is better at managing money. What will you teach your children about money? Most of what we learned about money will come from how we grew up. What was money like when you were growing up? If you had fiscally responsible parents who took time to teach you about money, then chances are you have a great foundation when it comes to finances if you follow their example and heed their advice.

If you don't want some of the same patterns you experienced in your childhood to be transferred to your children, then you and your husband will have to be on the same page and teach them the culture of spending that will yield them success in adulthood. Dave Ramsey, the founder of Financial Peace University, says that money management is 80% behavior and 20% head knowledge. Adults devise a plan and follow it, but kids do what feels good.[10] If you aren't on the same page with your finances, your marriage may not work.

Identify who is the saver and who is the spender. Some spenders are known for not having much when they were children; savers are usually the ones who don't ever want to be broke. Spenders may have been deprived of basic things and made inner vows to themselves that, when they grew up, things would be different. Savers don't ever want to be deprived of basic necessities. You need to understand why he does what he does with money.

A young lady came to me for counseling. Her husband was a spender and very fiscally irresponsible. Often, people who are spenders have credit and debt issues. While it is possible to be a "spender" and still pay the bills on time, this is not usually the case. For the husband in question, it was not his story.

To add to the dysfunction, he was stubborn and selfish. He didn't like to be told what to do. They had two different philosophies on money and how it should be managed. She was a saver and believed in having money for emergencies and major purchases. He pretty much lived in the moment and by the day. Understand going in that money fights and money differences are one of the biggest sources of contention in a marriage.

She was the one who officially handled the finances. However, her husband would withdraw funds from their joint checking account without checking with her—or verifying an available balance with the bank. Consequently, it was nothing for him to have incurred $200 or more in overdraft charges on a regular basis. When she tried to discuss it with him, he simply refused to cooperate with any plan at all.

She came to me at her wits' end; mentally and emotionally drained. As we began to chat, she mentioned that she saw this behavior in him before they got married but never deemed it as a "red flag." He would spend money without giving purchases a second thought. Being so young, she was without much wisdom in this area and just figured things would meld when they got married. She believed he would become fiscally responsible and see what needed to be done and just do it. Surprisingly, to her, this was not the case. He continued the irresponsible behavior several years into their marriage. Needless to say, they paid a lot of unnecessary interest on loans and had constant arguments and disagreements on money.

To the woman who will marry a man who likes to spend, hear me well. What you see will always be, and even more so, after marriage unless they allow God to change them. Money makes you a bigger person than you currently are. If he is a spender before you get married, he will be one afterwards. He may not have had proper guidance on money management issues. If he's a saver, investor, and wise with money, it will benefit you greatly. See it as a blessing.

Address any money issues in premarital counseling. Then, sit down with a financial planner who can work with you both to make sure you are on the same page. This is not an issue you can overlook. Excuses won't be good enough when you have spent and lived on everything you made and get to retirement with nothing, not to mention, still living in a rented apartment because of your failure to purchase your own home.

If you are the spender and have irresponsible spending behaviors, listen carefully. You cannot take this selfish attitude into your marriage. It will cost you in ways you cannot imagine. Changes in how you spend must be made when you are married. You may not be able to shop as much as you desire in the beginning, but it won't always be that way. Submit yourself to finding the rhythm of adjusting to married life and becoming one which requires patience, flexibility, and discipline. Gradually, you will be able to resume with purchases you enjoy.

If you need discipline with your own spending, start now. Ask a trusted friend or family member to keep you accountable. If you haven't already, start using a budget and stick with it. Spend every dollar on paper first, which means writing down all your expenses before paying them. Download a budget app onto your phone or tablet to track your expenses. If you are not willing to submit your spending habits and desires to work cohesively with your mate and make radical changes, then you aren't ready to be married. You wouldn't believe how many relationships have been destroyed because of money!

the beauty of purity

God created sex. It was His idea and a great one at that! He created it to be enjoyed within the relationship of husband and wife. In today's culture, waiting until marriage to enjoy sex is antiquated. It's rare, uncommon, and unheard of. We live in a hypersexual culture and the majority of sexually active people aren't married. The Bible is clear on God's stance on this topic, and He has not changed His mind regardless of what society says and does. It does not matter what anyone thinks. Sexual purity is one of God's commands to us. Period! 1 Thessalonians 4:3-5 (NASB) says, "It is God's will that you should be sanctified: that you should avoid sexual immorality; that each of you should learn to control his own body in a way that is holy and honorable, not in passionate lust like the heathen, who do not know God."

Some couples justify having sex before marriage stating that they plan to get married anyway. None of that changes the facts on what God said about marriage and how it sows seeds of destruction and insecurity in your relationship. Refraining from sex before marriage places you in a position where God can grace your life and marriage with His very best. God's promises are often conditional and must be accepted. They don't happen automatically. We have a part to play first.

One of the things I have discovered when mentoring women is how bad some of them feel about having had sex before they were married. They feel guilty and ashamed. They are caught in a cycle that they feel is virtually unbreakable. If this is you, know God does not condemn you and has forgiven you. The hard part will be you forgiving yourself. He loves you infinitely and will not hold any indiscretions against you. Allow the Holy Spirit to enable you to do what you can't do in your own strength. Make up in your mind, moving forward, that you won't give yourself away to any man but your husband. That includes not having sex until you are married; not just engaged. You are worth far more than giving benefits without a commitment.

Having sex before marriage changes how we feel about each other and weakens the relationship. Shanti Feldhahn, a ground-breaking social researcher and best-selling author, did a poll with a group of young people who had had sex before marriage. She asked them what happened as a result of them having sex before marriage. Of the men, 70% who had sex before marriage said they could no longer trust their girlfriend. Of the women, 82% who had sex before marriage became deeply insecure of the relationship, saying it caused them to become clingy and emotionally needy.[11]

So you may ask why would a man develop a lack of trust with his girlfriend after they've had sex? It's because he considers you easy. He just got everything you have to offer and wonders if you are giving it to anyone else. Even if, on some basic level, he knows that it is not true, the question seems to always be there.

One gentleman shared his personal opinion with me on the topic. He said most men would not commit to a girl who gave up sex too quickly, because they can't be trusted. He's wondering, if you gave it up easy to me, are you doing that with other men?

Women have a tendency to become insecure when they give a man all they have. The mystery is gone and cannot be recaptured. You have given him everything you have to give; you have nothing more to offer. When we wait until we get married, it creates trust in men and security in women the way God intended it to be.

A woman confided in me during a heart to heart conversation we were having about life and marriage in general. She shared that she and her husband, who had been married for over 15 years, did not wait until they were married before having sexual relations. To be honest with you, I was surprised to hear this particular couple didn't wait. You know when you think highly of someone and think, "Not them. Surely they honored God."

She continued to tell me she wished she could go back in time and remain celibate until they were married. Not only was there guilt and regret but also an insecurity that was instilled in her that comes along with having sex before marriage. She has to battle the thought of her husband not having the discipline to resist the temptation of sexual sin in the marriage relationship, because he didn't discipline himself before he was married to her.

Abstaining from sex is a discipline, and sexual purity does not end when you get married. Discipline still plays a part in not falling into sexual sin through adultery, pornography, and other lewd behavior. You will need to exercise self control many times and in many ways, not just sexually when you're married.

Maintaining discipline and honoring God's direction for our lives is the blessing of being able to stand at the altar on your wedding day, knowing you have been true to God's Word. It's realizing the blessing comes from choosing to walk a difficult path. I don't know anyone who doesn't want their marriage to be blessed by their obedience to walk in sexual purity. We can do it our way and get our results, or do it His way and get His rewards.

marriage is a marathon with no finish line

Preparing to run a marathon is arduous and painstaking. The physical agility and mental stamina it takes to finish the race is hard. Training occurs months in advance and requires consistency, endurance, and discipline. You will have to push yourself to keep going, yet the reward is the personal achievement that comes when you make it to the finish line.

While marriage is like a marathon, there is no finish line. It is consistency, pushing past trying times while also enjoying the great benefits that come with it. Marriage is not a destination; you never arrive. Rather, you grow deeper in love and experience more intimacy over time.

The love you have for each other now will in no way compare to what you will have in the years to come. It is only after your marriage has gone through some seasons and weathered some storms that you'll know and appreciate the depth of your love for each other. You can have a marriage that gets better and better and lasts a lifetime.

Marriage takes both individuals willing to die to themselves for the betterment of the relationship. It's not each of you giving 50/50, but rather each gives 100/100. It's about serving wholeheartedly, loving unconditionally, and forgiving repeatedly. None of this is predicated on how you feel. Just like training for a marathon, you can't quit because it hurts; you must push through it and keep going. It takes what it takes. You signed up for "until death do you part," not until "I'm tired of this!"

Marriage takes intentionality. You must both be intentional about working through differences and learning how to fight fair, dismantling unrealistic expectations, and fighting for your marriage. You must cover your husband with love, care, concern and prayer. The two of you must be a unified front against anything that would come against you as individuals and against your marriage.

There will be times you will have to fight through hardships to keep going. I would be remiss if I didn't share with you the fact that you have an enemy who hates marriage and will stop at nothing to destroy yours. You and your husband will have to cover your family in prayer to ward off the fiery darts the enemy will throw trying to obliterate your relationship.

John 10:10 tells us the enemy comes to steal, kill, and destroy. He has no desire to see one person fulfill a purpose, much less the mathematical, unbelievable things that God does with a union of two. The devil is the enemy, not your husband. Always remember that! The fight is for your family, because the family is the social fabric that holds society together. It's what makes society work. This is why the enemy hates it and will stop at nothing to destroy yours.

If you allow the enemy to deceive you into thinking otherwise, his mission will be accomplished. Settle it in your mind now that you will win the war that is waged against marriages. You will not be a negative statistic.

I admit there are some heavy subject matters discussed in this book. Some of which is why many marriages fail. Almost everyone gets married with the best of intentions. I can't think of one person who went into their marriage wanting it to fail. Throw a second marriage with a blended family in the mix, and the stakes are even higher. For third marriages, the majority of those don't make it.

But we are not without hope! In Christ you can do this.

Yes, it is going to be work, and there will be challenges, but, even more so, there will be wonderful times as well. Challenges are a part of being human; we all have them. With the Holy Spirit guiding and preparing you, He will help you, but will only to the extent to which you allow Him.

Marriage is an institution created by God. He is the mastermind behind it and also knows how it works best. Why wouldn't you look to the Designer to find out how He intended for it to work? Marriage is not a do-it-yourself project. Allow the Architect to help you build something wonderful in your relationship.

Yes, marriage is work, but the rewards are profound and abundant. More than anything, it requires you to be in the face of the Lord, praying and asking for His wisdom and guidance. You need Him to be at the center of your relationship as He is the anchor for it to last 10, 25, or 50+ years.

practical steps to becoming wife ready

1. Create a daily habit of devotions with prayer and reading your Bible. The blueprint for being a wife can be found in God's Word.

2. Start developing the fruits of the Spirit (Galatians 5:22-23). Ask the Holy Spirit to reveal the areas where you fall short.

3. Pursue sexual purity at all costs.

afterword

In closing, I would like to leave you with this. To the women who are not married yet, you may be wondering, "If I'm doing all of this to get ready, what about him? What steps will my future mate be taking, because the work goes both ways." And you are right, it does. When you have taken the steps to become whole and ready for marriage, God won't bless you with anything less. He is too good, mindful, and faithful for that. His desire is two whole individuals; not fragments of who you truly are, coming together to become one flesh. And you'll have a greater awareness having read this book.

While you must believe God is preparing a man who will be tailor-made for you, you can begin now praying for him. Ask God to send godly men into his life, who will hold him accountable and help him be that strong man after His own heart. You want a mate who loves God more than he loves you! Pray for his concerns and any fears he has about leading a family. Pray about his goals and dreams. Pray that any past family issues are resolved. Pray that when you meet for the first time, there will be an unction in your spirit, so you'll both know you are each other's God-ordained mate. There are so many things you can be in prayer about before you know who he is, and there is no better time than now to begin.

For those who are currently married, you may have identified some of the issues in this book as problematic in your relationship. Take heart! It's never too late to work through them. If you haven't already, find a Christian marriage counselor who can walk you through those areas. You and your husband should go together for optimum results. However, if he chooses not to, go alone. Your marriage can be helped immensely if you initiate change. You cannot change your spouse, but you can change yourself.

When you make positive changes, it allows positive changes to occur in your spouse. 1 Peter 3:1-2 (NASB) says, "In the same way, you wives, be submissive to your own husbands so that even if any *of them* are disobedient to the word, they may be won without a word by the behavior of their wives, as they observe your chaste and respectful behavior." Sometimes the best way to change your spouse is to model positive changes in your own life. You can do that without saying a word.

Perhaps you are divorced and desire to be remarried. It's a great desire to have. Marriage works if you work at it, and perhaps you or your ex-husband weren't willing to work through some issues. It truly takes both individuals working together.

I want to encourage you to take the necessary time and steps to get healed and whole. Don't rush into the next relationship. Take some time getting to know yourself again and what you like, need, and love. Refuse to settle. Refuse to compromise. Dismantle limiting beliefs that may be lingering from the stench of your divorce, which has challenged your thinking on what you deserve. You owe it to yourself to be restored, fulfilled, and happy. Marriage won't make you happy; you will make marriage happy.[12]

The marriage relationship is wonderful, romantic, exciting, rewarding, and life-giving. I highly recommend all women to experience it. There is nothing on earth like being in love with the love of your life.

While no one can be fully prepared, because no one is perfect, you can be better prepared. Do all you can to be healed and whole on this side of "I do." That way, or in doing so, when the time comes for you join your life with your God-sent mate, you will be ready to build your relationship on a firm foundation.

about the author

Kim McQuitty is an author, speaker, mentor, and premarital counselor, who has been encouraging women through ministry for over 25 years. She challenges and inspires them to maximize their potential and walk in their God-appointed purpose by fulfilling Christ's mandate for their lives. Many have been touched by her pragmatic, influential messages that transform lives, heal hearts, and win souls for Jesus Christ. Her vision is for ordinary women to become extraordinary women of distinction, worth, emotional wholeness, and Kingdom excellence.

Through her commitment in helping women and her passion for marriage, Kim founded Wife

Ready Boot Camp, an intensive workshop to help women prepare for marriage beyond the wedding day. Her mission is to equip and empower women, impart wisdom, and practical habits to them so they can become better prepared for the marathon of marriage. She resides in Atlanta, GA and has 2 adult daughters.

wife ready boot camp

Wife Ready Boot Camp is a life-changing seminar for women who desire marriage, are engaged, or are newly married. During this time, we will be:

- uncovering the dynamics that interfere with having a happy and healthy relationship

- sharing tools for conflict resolution and overcoming communication challenges

- getting to the root of repeated relationship mistakes

- challenging and empowering single and newly married women to take an honest look at themselves

- providing education about the marriage covenant, and the commitment and sacrifices involved

- shedding light on the main issues that causes marriages to fail

Participants will receive advice from marriage counselors, seasoned married couples, and relationship coaches to help them enter into marriage as "ready" and prepared as possible. To bring *Wife Ready* Boot Camp to your city, community or church, simply log onto www. wifeready.org and complete the Boot Camp Booking

Inquiries section to receive more information.

end notes

[1] *Kingdom Woman: Embracing Your Purpose, Power, and Possibilities*, by Tony Evans and Chrystal Evans Hurst, Tyndale House Publishers, Inc., 2015, p. 154.

[2] Stanley, Scott M., et al. "Communication, Conflict, and Commitment: Insights on the Foundations of Relationship Success from a National Survey." Freshwater Biology, Wiley/Blackwell (10.1111), 8 Sept. 2004, snd to which organization they are owede.ually they called it off. kes to be fully whole... od. (remove all dashes)love, life an

[3] "Expensive Weddings Are More Likely To End In Divorce, Study Finds." Business 2 Community, Business 2 Community, www.business2community.com/social-buzz/expensive-weddings-are-more-likely-to-end-in-divorce-study-finds-01034565.

[4] "10 Surprising Facts About Loneliness." Psychology Today, Sussex Publishers, www.psychologytoday.com/us/blog/the-squeaky-wheel/201410/10-surprising-facts-about-loneliness.

[5] *Date or Soul Mate?: How to Know If Someone Is Worth Pursuing in Two Dates or Less*, by Dr. Neil Clark Warren, Thomas Nelson Publishers, 2002, p. 100.

[6] 21 Day Journey, 21dayjourney.com.

[7] "Practical Tips for Staying in Love | MarriageToday | Jimmy Evans." MarriageToday, 20 Dec. 2016, www.youtube.com/watch?v=BFrkG7aLQzc.

[8] "What Premarital Counseling Research Says." Premarital Counseling San Diego, 25 Oct. 2012, premaritalcounseling-sandiego.com/premarital-counseling/what-premarital-counseling-research-says.

[9] "Pre-Marriage Counseling - Facilitators." SYMBIS Assessment, www.symbis.com/facilitators.

[10] Ramsey, Dave. "The Cure for Excessive Spending." Daveramsey.com, Ramsey Solutions, 1 Dec. 2017, www.daveramsey.com/blog/the-cure-for-excessive-spending.

[11] "Research and Surveys." Shaunti Feldhahn, shaunti.com/research.

[12] *Save Your Marriage Before It Starts*, by Les Parrott and Leslie Parrott, Zondervan, 1995, p. 83

Made in the USA
Columbia, SC
23 November 2018